the rounds

joseph zitt

the apocryphile press

BERKELEY, CA

www.apocryphile.org

apocryphile press
BERKELEY, CA

Apocryphile Press
1700 Shattuck Ave #81
Berkeley, CA 94709
www.apocryphile.org

Printed in the United States of America
ISBN 1-933993-70-7

the rounds

joseph zitt

To the good people and pets of
Grace North Church
and the other
citizens, denizens, and residents
of Berkeley, California

Prologue
2:42 AM, 15 Dec 2006

A small truck barreled down my street a moment ago, barely missing a couple of deer. The guy at the corner with the iPod headphones noticed it coming, fortunately, and stopped. Even more fortunately, the person pushing an overloaded shopping cart had already gotten across—that cart speeds up, slows, and stops for no one, save, perhaps, for the dictates of the person that we can't see, with whom the person with the cart (gender unknown) always seems to be arguing.

Our street is the only straight path from the hills down to the bay. Vehicles moving too quickly down it often lose their brakes on the steep, slick street, and hope that their horns will keep the path clear until they can stop. The horns threaten to wake the monks downstairs from me.

Me, I'm a night-owl. Once I manage to fall asleep, I can sleep through anything.

Here, in this neighborhood spanning the space between the Gourmet Ghetto and Holy Hill, it seems like every other building is either an Internet coffee joint or a church. The Graduate Theological Union, a few blocks away, up a daunting climb from here, combines several disparate seminaries and schools of divinity and religion on one campus. A variety of churches, synagogues, community centers, religious schools, and yoga rooms fan out from there, with a mosque, Zen center, Jewish meditation center, and other sites on the far side of the University campus.

Students are everywhere. Most, it seems, are per-

petually either on cellphones or iPods as they walk. When they gather in the coffee shops, they open their laptops and act as if no one else is around. With each staring into his or her own screen, it seems as if they are in a networked game of Battleship. At least it seems that way to me, since I'm old enough to remember when Battleship was popular and personal computers hadn't yet been released.

There's something about cities like this, towns that the residents jokingly call "The People's Republic of" whatever the name of the place is, that draws the odd people in. The mad geniuses, the hackers, the seekers, the troubled, those who have a sense that there's more to the world than what they see, and those who see things and hear voices that the rest of us can't, all seem drawn to Austin, to Boulder, to Takoma Park, and here to Berkeley, in search (conscious or not) of something that they often cannot name.

I got here in 2002, driving straight out Interstate 80 from where it starts in New Jersey to where it ends, and going directly to a barbecue for the Fourth of July. After twenty years working with computers in various ways, and after being laid off by a confused and delusional dot.com, I was ready for something new.

I moved in with friends, in this community above the monks, and half-heartedly looked for more computer work. I eventually lucked into an utterly unrelated job as Classical Music Guy at a large record store (earning a quarter of what I had gotten in the dot.com days, but infinitely happier with my job). But with the insane expenses of Bay Area life, it wasn't enough to live on.

And then, by chance or grace, a second job came to me, offered by a friend with the right connections and a good sense of matching needs and skills. And I got to know more of the neighborhood, and specifically of one church down the road, than I ever thought that I would have.

And, as I had been doing for several years, I wrote everything down in my blog (http://blog.joseph zitt.com/). Here's a small subset of what I wrote, drawn from there, and edited somewhat to focus on the church job and the multifaceted neighborhood in which I live.

4:09 PM, 11 Mar 2003

As of a few nights ago, I'm "security guy" at the church around the corner from where I live. This means that each night, I go around the exterior and interior of the church and make sure that all the right doors and windows are open, locked, or ajar, and that the right lights and fans are on or off, as well as that there aren't any vagrants about.

A guy who lived in a room in the church basement had held the position for the past seven years, but he's now moving on. Since he can be odd and abrasive, the original plan was that I wouldn't be introduced to him, and would just pick up when he stopped. As it turns out, it's taking much longer for him to move out than planned (he's an incredible packrat, with a huge amount of broken electronics and the like in his room), so I've run across him just about every night.

Fortunately, and to the amazement and pleasure of the other folks at the church, he and I are getting along quite well, and I'm, effectively, training for the position under him. He's been showing me how he does things in (perhaps too much) detail, and explaining his view of the various people (church officers, space renters, neighbors, and police) that I'll encounter. And on several nights he has done the rounds again after I've done them, and noted things that I could do better. So it's coming together well. And I'm learning more than I ever wanted to know about church organization and architecture: I can now identify the nave, narthex, and sacristy, and understand why it's so odd that the church is a Congregational church with an Anglican liturgy.

The church has a very good piano, which I have access to on off hours. I'd been wanting to teach myself harmony this year, so I'm looking forward to sitting down at the piano with a good textbook (I've been enjoying reading Schoenberg's *Theory of Harmony*) and working my way through it. Harmony has always been my weak point, and I've never quite gotten how it works. For one thing, root position major triads always sound sort of wrong to me at the piano, as if they want to resolve to something else. But I was reminded last night of what I wanted to learn when I happened to hear the Jackson 5's "I'll Be There" and was grabbed by some marvelous chords in it that I couldn't identify other than as beautiful blurs.

4:08 PM, 12 Mar 2003

I got more pointers last night as I did my rounds at the church. My predecessor had spotted some more details re: how I positioned some of the doors and showed up to show me how he does it. And, as is his wont, to regale me with his life stories and talk about the church folk, etc, for an hour.

One pleasing thing, in view of how tense the relationship between him and the people running the church had become: he told me that the extended sessions of talking with me had helped to dissipate much of his anger and ill will toward the folks in charge, and made it easier to leave in a less hostile mood. He's acknowledged that I seem to have learned the job well and that he's leaving the building in good hands.

1:59 PM, 13 Mar 2003

Last night I met the leader of the Liberal Catholic congregation that holds services on Saturdays at the church. Their service, which involves a lot of iconography and ritual objects, has roots in Theosophy and other related stuff that I didn't quite follow at first explanation.

He's very quiet, and opening communications with him was slow. While we were sitting in the sacristy, though, a spider gradually lowered itself from the ceiling to hang at eye level between us. We observed it for a while, and I told him a story that I had heard from Jewish folklore about King David and a spider. He responded with a story about Jacob sleeping under the stars. From that, we broke the ice and got to talking quite avidly. It was a very "Darmok and Jilad at Tanagra" moment.

I also ran into my predecessor, who is still moving out of the church. He had just put out an immense number of bagged items to be picked up by recycling in the morning. (Faced with an daunting mess, he found a way to start cleaning by first pulling together all the "mixed paper" in the room, then all the recyclable plastics, etc.) He also showed me some obscure doors that I hadn't known about before, and how to check them.

10:08 PM, 15 Mar 2003

I find myself facing a quandary.

On most week days, several people have lunch on the church steps. Yesterday I contemplated introducing myself as the church's security guy, giving them my card, and asking them to let me know if they spot anything worrisome going on. But then I wondered what the parameters of "worrisome" might be, and if I weren't thinking of asking for just the kind of citizen surveillance that we complain about when the government requests it.

The job is going increasingly smoothly. I now have keys and codes to all the places that I need to check, and have charted a simple path through the church that hits all the spots. The biggest delay is encountering my talkative predecessor, who tends to trap me for an hour at a time in his stream of consciousness. But he'll be gone after tomorrow night.

2:00 PM, 17 Mar 2003

I've spent the last hour and a half (counting from when I'm first writing this sentence) down at the intersection at the northeast corner of this block, standing quietly, holding a candle, together with over fifty of my neighbors and expected thousands (hundreds of thousands?) of people around the world in another symbolic action for peace.

We gathered at about 7 PM outside the church next door (not the one across the street where I work). Some church members, children, and a monk from downstairs in his official robes distributed small candles in well-designed disposable holders. Some other people arrived with their own candles. Working outward from the center, people lit their candles from others' and offered their own flames to light those of people who had come later, as well as those that went out in the gentle breeze.

The group separated to stand at the four corners of the intersection. (The local organizer, with whom I stood, hadn't planned this, but was pleased when it happened spontaneously.) There were more than a dozen of us in our cluster of people, and I saw as many or more flames at each of the other corners, with many more at the church itself.

While some vigils had been planned to be silent, ours wasn't: people talked quietly among themselves, mostly about the war and about what we had been hearing on the Net and in the media, and wondering about upcoming actions. I met several neighbors that I hadn't seen before, as well as some folks who had come from greater distances. Many of them had passed other vigils, most apparently even larger than ours, within a couple of miles of here.

Not much happened, as we expected. There was a lot more traffic at this corner than I had thought that there would be, and many of the passing cars, stopping at the four-way stop sign, honked their horns or flashed their lights at us (in agreement, we hope). Candles went out and were lit again, the flame moving from candle to candle. (Later on, a woman showed up with a long flint-based device for lighting fireplaces. It proved a more effective tool than other candles, so people came to her for relighting.) Passersby passed by. Some nodded, some asked what was going on, some moved carefully around or through the crowd, and some joined us, going across the street for candles or accepting them from people who offered theirs then retrieved new ones. People took photos with digital cameras, which they promised to upload to the Net sites collecting images.

By 8:15, most of the uniform candles had gone out, and people dispersed. I was among the last to leave, and headed upstairs to write this.

I note less optimistically that my car was broken into last night in our parking lot. There was no visible damage, but the glove compartment and trunk were both open when I came down this morning. I hadn't kept much in the car, because I knew that this might happen. I think the thief got my sleeping bag and my inflatable air mattress (though I may have that stashed somewhere around here indoors), as well as some small tools (hammers, screwdrivers, sandpaper, etc) left over from a woodworking project last year.

Fortunately none of it was particularly expensive nor necessary. I'm not happy that this happened, but not as upset as I might otherwise be.

2:44 PM, 20 Mar 2003

My predecessor is finally gone from the church, after taking much longer than he expected. The curtains are down from his windows, and his room is pretty much clear. He's said that anything he's left behind is open for scavenging; I may cobble together some computer gear. He left a huge amount of stuff to be picked up by recycling.

As he thought might happen, they took everything except a large bag of plastic bags. I saw it as I headed past toward the coffee shops, so I scooped it up and brought it to the local supermarket where they recycle plastic bags. There were too many to fit in their container, but they said that I could just leave my bag of bags next to it, where it would be picked up within an hour. (With my ongoing awareness of possibilities for bombs, I would have been leery of letting anyone deposit a large opaque object in a public place, but they apparently weren't worried.)

5:13 PM, 26 Mar 2003

Last night I actually got around to doing my rounds while not yet dog-tired, so I took a moment to pause in the nave (that's the main part of the sanctuary) to play the piano there. When I looked at the clock, two hours had shot past. I had stumbled across some chords that I liked, and a rather Keith Jarrett-like melody appeared above them, which I played and improvised on, then wrote down (slowly—I find that it takes me a long time to notate music, since I keep forgetting what I did once I've written down a few notes, and have to figure it out all over again).

There was a fatal crash yesterday morning outside the Priory where I live. From what I understand, a delivery-sized truck hit a jeep or SUV and a traffic light, then landed on its side, killing the driver. The other driver was able to get out of her vehicle and was taken to a hospital. I, of course, slept right through all the crashing, sirens, etc, and only found out what little I know later in the day. This morning there was a single wine bottle with carefully arrayed flowers in it at the point of impact.

4:55 PM, 27 Mar 2003

We had an unsettling visitor last night as I was cooking dinner. I first heard the banging coming from the door to another unit, down the balcony from our kitchen, then on our own door. When I looked outside, no one was there, but I saw an unkempt man was talking, from the middle of the balcony, to the resident of the apartment at the far end. I closed the kitchen door and went back to cooking.

After a few moments, the banging at our door resumed. When I opened the door, the same man was standing there. He spoke slowly: "Peace and love ...neighbor...would you have...a book of matches?" Now, maybe I'm absorbing the paranoia from my predecessor at the church job, but there was no way that I was going to trust someone I didn't know with a book of matches—especially since it was recycling night, and all along the sidewalks were paper bags full of more paper and other containers full of flammable plastics (including a large batch propped up against a wooden pillar of the church). I told him that no one at our house smoked, so we didn't have any matches. He nodded and again said "Peace and love...." and continued to stand there until I closed the door.

My neighbor down the balcony was quite perturbed by this. If he shows up again, she's going to call the cops.

4:57 PM, 2 Apr 2003

Last night, as I was doing my rounds, a small, beautiful, brown and white shelled snail dropped from above a door to the ground when the door shut. I picked it up, and feeling the snail's movement within the shell, realized that it was alive, so I carefully placed it in the garden.

1:53 AM, 5 Sep 2003

When I ran into one of the priests from the church last weekend, he said it was hard to tell whether I was actually doing that job, since there was rarely anyone there when I came through, and I rarely reported problems. This is the constant paradox of the watchman: when we do our job well, it's hard to tell that we are doing it at all.

This makes me not as sure as some that our National Security policies aren't doing any good, though I remain extremely wary of the way that human rights are being trampled in our name; we rarely would hear about crimes that are prevented, either through the measures foiling them or through the potential criminals being deterred from planning them in the first place.

I told him some ways that he could tell that I was doing my work: in each of the three spaces that I check, I change the state of at least one item from how people leave them at the end of the day. I suppose that the more certain way of doing things would be to have a log sheet of some sort in each space. But fortunately the folks at the church are more trusting than that.

Which reminds me that I have to get some pliers on the way home so I can stop by the church and replace the broken toilet seat in one of the bathrooms. The seat had split, the front half of the oval snapping right off. I'm baffled as to how that could have happened. The folks at the church had left me a note asking me to replace it, along with the new seat and a pointer to some tools...but not pliers.

10:42 PM, 11 Sep 2003

Most nights, on my rounds in the church, I pause in the nave, sit down in the pews, and think through the day. Picking up on something I learned from the liturgy of Tom's church, I look at what I've done and experienced, either as things that I give thanks for or things that I see could be improved. And part of it is to ask myself if things in the world are, in whatever small way (akin to the shift of air from a butterfly's wing?), better than they were when I woke up. Most days I'm pleased to see things balance favorably, even if it boils down to making someone happy by finding him the Ray Conniff record that he grew up with.

Some might file these thoughts as "prayer." I finesse the issue by not worrying about that. (But then why am I writing about it?) The thanks and requests for improvement are certainly not directed to an anthropomorphic God, but more toward myself and outward in a less specific way. This relates to the refrain from the book my parents read to me (Dorothy Karp Kripke's *Let's Talk About God*): "God is the good that's in the world."

I experienced my first earthquake last Thursday evening. Several of us were in the Priory common room when the building gave a small thump. It felt like a large air conditioning system shuddering to a halt, or like a subway was passing underneath. A few minutes later, there was another, smaller thump. We all wondered if that had been an earthquake, since none of us had ever felt one, and it felt too small to count.

2:11 AM, 3 Oct 2003

Along the path that I walk to the church, just before I get there, a tree arches over the sidewalk, slightly higher than I am tall. The tree has had fragrant flowers for months now; their scent precedes it by a few feet. Even when I'm lost in thought, the scent lets me know that it's time to dig out my keys and flashlight and to set my mind to my rounds.

2:36 AM, 24 Jan 2004

As I walk past the church, I see a shopping cart full of odd objects parked under the arch that leads to the back walkway. Next to it, boxes have been set up as a makeshift and sturdy-looking bed, with a plastic bag stuffed with other plastic bags placed at one end as a pillow. Though I feel compassion for their owner (and some admiration for the improvised workmanship), I can't let it remain there.

I don't have time to do anything about it on the way to my primary job, so I call my main contact on the church board. She tells me that my predecessor used

to dismantle these installations and discard them, but agrees that I can let it stay until I do my rounds tonight (around 1 AM).

I'm not looking forward to the possible confrontation; if I sense any danger, I'll just hand the problem off to the police. My impulse is to gently awaken the person by shining my flashlight at him, tell him that he has to move on, tell him that if the objects are there in the morning, they'll be discarded, and leave. This may be the most effective yet face-saving compromise. (A sudden thought: near the archway, I saw an old and scruffy woman pruning the plants near the curb and muttering to herself. Could the objects be hers?)

At the corner of Shattuck and Addison at 2:30 PM, I see seven bicycles, four parked and three in motion. A bearded man in tattered clothes moans, repeatedly and wordlessly, into the receiver of a pay phone.

As I walk down Shattuck Street, a man walks past me hissing "Bad spirits! Bad, bad, bad, bad spirits! Spirits! Bad, bad spirits!" A few minutes later, another man in a wheelchair rumbles past me in the opposite direction, hoarsely shouting "Bombard China!" As I watch him, a grey-haired man, his beard much wider than his face, crouches close to the ground on my right and looks up at me, then suddenly springs upright and trots away.

As I wait for the BART, the guy next to me on a concrete bench startles me by suddenly shouting "Checkmate!" I look over at him. Grinning, he shows me his cell phone. The screen shows a chessboard, perhaps an inch tall. "I got mate in ten minutes!" he says. I smile back and nod as he flips the phone shut and puts it away. I wonder if the stereo earphones that he wears are connected to it or to another, hidden device.

Doing my church rounds on the way home, I see the shopping cart still in the archway, but emptied. Most of the boxes are gone, and the few that remain appear strewn about. There is no sign of whoever constructed the site. I wouldn't have expected to see the shopping cart empty. I hope that this doesn't mean that someone has discarded or destroyed all of a homeless person's remaining belongings. I email the church folk to ask them if they know, and wonder what I will learn.

3:03 AM, 16 Feb 2004

Doing my rounds at 2 AM, I found that one of the pilot lights for the church kitchen's stove was out and re-lit it. I then ran cold water over the smoldering tip of the long wooden match to quench the flame. The impact made a long hissing sound that got louder then softer, seemingly in time to the splatting of the drops of water on the metal sink.

3:24 AM, 24 Feb 2004

As I came up the escalator from the Downtown Berkeley BART station, I saw that the standard vandals had been at work on the McDonald's billboard that is always in view as I ride up to the street. The vandals are meticulous, pasting revisions of the ad slogans in a similar font, so you have to look twice to realize that something's wrong. Last month, the slogan "Suddenly you're a morning person" became "Suddenly you're not a person." Tonight, "The feel good menu of the year" had become "The foul food menu of the year." To my surprise, the last revision had been left there until the billboard changed completely. On the other hand, the vandalizing might have been to McDonald's' benefit: if it weren't for the alteration, I might never have noticed—and certainly wouldn't have remembered—what the original ad slogan had been.

Much of downtown Berkeley was dark, with the power mysteriously shut down. I walked down University Avenue without the help of streetlights. The headlights from passing cars and the bright gleam of the still-functioning traffic lights made it possible for me to see. Still, were I not a rather large man, I would have been worried about the safety of walking the block alone.

As I approached Au Coquelet, I remembered that I had a flashlight on me (as I almost always do, for my rounds at the church), took it out, and turned it on. At the same moment, another man (also heavyset, bearded, and in a light parka) turned his flashlight on, illuminating the front of the restaurant which, like every-

thing else on the block, was closed.

"Any idea what's with the power?" I asked.

He shook his head. "I hoped you'd know. Everything's down for a few blocks in any direction, though some stuff's on." He waved his flashlight at several buildings where faint glows shone from the lobbies.

"Security lights, on batteries?" I guessed.

He looked at them and nodded. "Looks like it's been a while, since stuff's had time to close down. But I don't know what caused it." He paused and waved his flashlight around vaguely. "Supposed to be weather coming in tonight, big wind and a rainstorm, so you'd think it would fail then. But maybe it's good it's shut down before then. Gives them time to fix it."

I nodded. "Well, off to someplace else then." He nodded back and we wandered off in our separate directions. He headed west on University toward the lights that shone past MLK. I went north on Milvia, then east on whatever is due north of University, where I saw that lights were on up near Shattuck. I ended up at Thai Noodle, which was crowded and noisier than usual, probably due to diners who would otherwise have been at Au Coquelet. I ate there, jittery and fidgeting, then did my rounds at the church. As I walked, some light rain began to fall, but in the few hours since then it hasn't developed into anything like the feared storm.

During my rounds, I found myself walking more loudly than usual, my footsteps reverberating in the newly uncarpeted nave. A few times, I did some exuberant stomping about, like a hippo auditioning for *Riverdance*, though I stopped when I thought I heard something at the far side of the room falling over in rhythm with my feet.

As I went through the Parish Hall, I discovered that twirling my flashlight around, as if I were vertically beating an egg, illuminated more of the room than keeping it steady, persistence of vision making it seem that a hollow oval of light was catching much of the far wall.

3:40 AM, 2 Mar 2004

Something went haywire with the audible traffic signals at Central and Shattuck tonight. While the traffic lights in both directions looked as they should, and the sound for crossing in one direction (I forget which) was behaving properly, the sound in the other had gotten chaotic. The lights usually chirp in loping rhythms from the poles on either side of the street, out of sync and slightly out of phase. Tonight, the far sound seemed to be taking improvised solos. Clusters of chirps sputtered out at arbitrary volumes, separated by silences of arbitrary durations and the occasional long tone, all at the usual pitch. It was far more interesting to hear than the standard sounds, though it might have conveyed less information or, even worse, erroneous news to those who needed to understand it.

3:14 AM, 9 Mar 2004

As I came up out of the BART this evening, I heard some odd percussion. I guessed that it wasn't any of the usual street musicians, since the playing was slightly unsteady and wasn't loud enough to attract most people's attention.

As I crossed Center Street, I saw the source of the sound: in front of the ATM machines at the bank, a man in a shabby green parka was bent over a translucent plastic bag, his knees straight but his head nearly touching the ground. With two sticks, he was tapping on a variety of objects (cans, bottles, cups) within the bag of trash. As I grew closer, what I had heard as unsteadiness in his playing revealed itself as the result of tricky overlapping phrases with different meters and dynamics, merging into a whole that was hard to follow when not heard as its individual pieces. The percussionist didn't have a cup or box out for donations and didn't seem to notice the other people around him. He continued, lost in his own complex soundscapes, as I walked away and lost his music in the noise of the street.

A few blocks down, a couple staggered past, tightly embracing, giggling and talking in what sounded like Japanese. Both seemed drunk past the point of being able to walk on only two legs. Their four-legged collaboration remained sufficiently upright though, lurching and tilting forward as each gingerly thrust feet ahead, each time barely keeping from falling over completely. They seemed to have hit a useful rhythm in their movement down the street. I suspect that they'd had lots of practice in learning to walk like this.

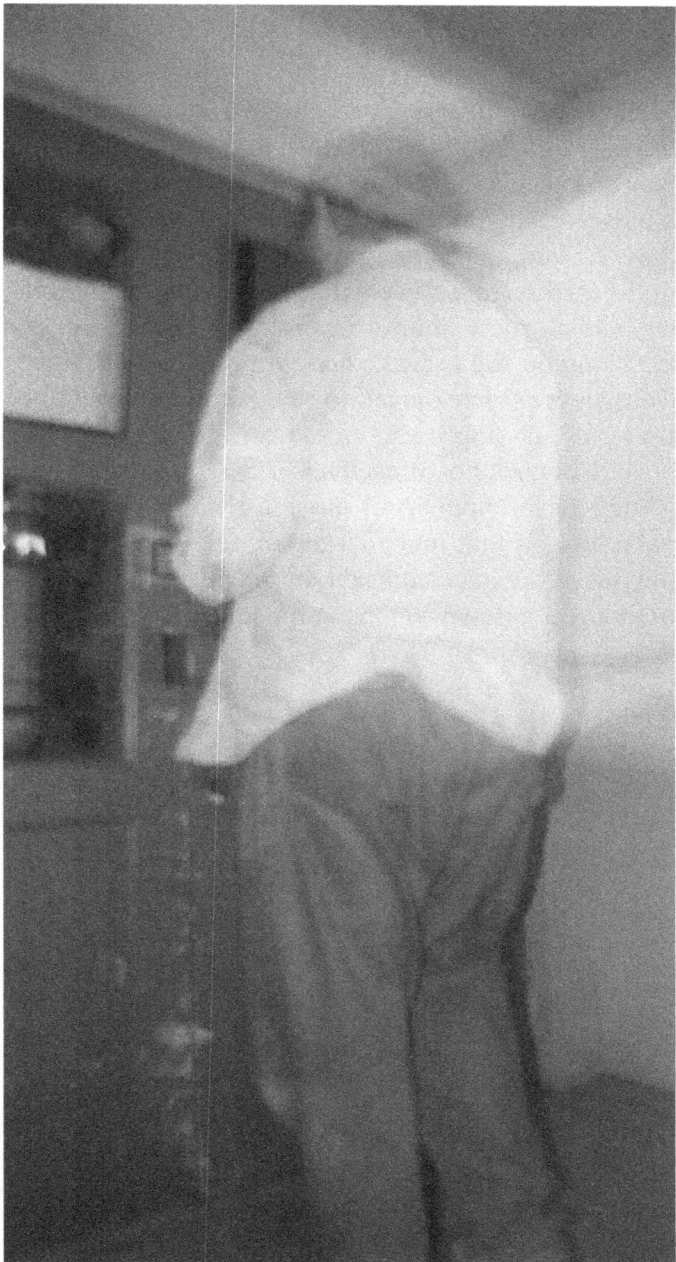

Down near Hearst Street, three young people (Cal undergraduates?) walked close to the buildings along Shattuck. Two held long slats with large wooden hands, each about three feet wide at the ends. As they moved along the street, they reached with the hands up toward second story windows, waving them in the air outside the windows from which light shone and knocking on the others, then withdrawing the hands from view as they darted to the next windows. When they saw me approach, one lowered his hand, brandished it in front of himself like a javelin, and bellowed "Gimme five, man!" As I passed, I slapped my open palm against that much larger wooden one. The people raised the hands upright on the poles and pumped them up and down, yelling in unison "Yes!"

2:31 AM, 10 Mar 2004

As I approached University Avenue today on the way to the BART, I saw a man in a wheelchair shuffle into the street at the beginning of a walk light, the chair moving inches as a time as his feet pushed against the asphalt. Before he was very far across, the light changed, but he continued his journey, gradually, inexorably, seeming to pay no attention to the traffic that was maneuvering around him. As he reached the other side, the light turned green again, and those of us who were waiting started to cross, only barely avoiding being hit by a huge truck that decided that it, too, would proceed despite the lights.

As the man crossed, I considered darting forward, grabbing the handles of the chair, and pushing him the rest of the way at an appropriate speed. But my usual indecision was increased by my bafflement as to the social protocols, as well as the possibility that the acceleration, if his feet were touching the ground, might propel him out of the chair entirely.

I was reminded of an Israeli programmer with whom I worked in Brooklyn many years ago. Seeing the traffic patterns in the neighborhood of the office, he said that he now understood that the traffic laws in the US seemed to be not rules but suggestions.

1:16 AM, 13 Mar 2004

On the way back from Saul's Deli, I stopped at a supermarket for some groceries. The man ahead of me in line was buying several bottles of wine and some frozen shrimp. He swiped his ATM card and punched in numbers, then headed out. The cashier saw that the PIN number didn't work, and called out to him to come back. He didn't stop, but when the guard gently blocked his way, he returned. His face, which looked sunburned within the hood of his parka (yes, even at 70 degrees F, many of the homeless and otherwise unusual people around here wear parkas), was streaming with tears.

It took a few more explanations by the cashier and guard before he seemed to understand. He produced his card and punched in the numbers, his shaking hand guiding the wand unsteadily, and again failed. The cashier asked him if he'd like to try one more time. He moaned, curled over, his head dropping deeply into the cart, sneezed several times, then, crying even harder, took the wand in both hands and punched the numbers, this time correctly.

When I got outside, I saw him tying the shopping bag to the handlebars of his bicycle. After I had walked about a block from the store, I heard his moaning yelp, which I now recognized, coming up to one side of me. I stepped to his other side, but he unsteadily cycled over in the direction in which I had stepped and threaded the gap between my arm and the wall, then continued bicycling, erratically, hazardously, and illegally, down the sidewalk. About a block past that, he passed me again on the other side of the street. He wasn't alone: another man in a matching shabby parka was walking the bicycle, his arm around the shopper, who had his head bowed and was walking gingerly, the friend keeping him from staggering into the street.

A little later, when I did my rounds, I came upon a mother and daughter unlocking their bicycles from the railing at the church. My ubiquitous flashlight came in handy as they pulled their gear together and rode off.

Down the stairs from them, I came upon a man sleeping in the shadows, his deep blue parka wrapped around him, and a rather new backpack under his head. When I shone the flashlight on his face, his eyes snapped open and he growled like a large dog. I stepped around him and went into the child care center. Not being in a mood for a confrontation, I ended up just stepping around him again as I left, making extremely sure that all entrances to the church were secure. If he's there tomorrow, I will have to call the police, but I decided, as I usually do the first time that I find someone there, to leave him for the single night in the relative shelter of the grounds.

10:09 PM, 18 Mar 2004

It's only about 70 degrees F here in town, but from within my room it feels like the city is melting. I'm sitting now at the French Hotel, a coffee shop near home, having scraped together enough dimes from my jar of coins (the quarters having already been consumed—I get paid overnight tonight, but am down to bare metal right now) to sit down with an iced coffee. This both gives me a comfortable place to write and gets me needed caffeine. Making coffee at home would, of course, be more economical, but in trying to prepare some while already jittery a few days ago, I smashed my french press and haven't gotten a new one yet.

The coffee shop is almost full, but doesn't feel crowded. The overhead radio is softly playing an oldies station. Until a moment ago, a woman at the next table was playing her acoustic guitar, working out a Brazilian-tinged arrangement of "Autumn Leaves" without regard to the music on the radio. As she packed up, two men walked in with their own guitars, each in what looked like expensive, sturdy cases. The woman and the men didn't appear to notice each other.

In the light beaming in through the door, I see a constellation of tiny flies hovering in slowly changing configurations. A bulldog, who has just dragged its owner into the shop, stares at them intently, as if waiting for them to line up perfectly for his attack.

At the counter, a pair of young women are peppering the cashier with questions: is the house coffee organic? (Yes.) Is it free trade? (He doesn't know.) The tiny blonde woman in the black sleeveless top and bright red Aztec-print shirt, carrying a fur-collared

leather jacket, appears convinced. It takes a bit longer for the tall brunette with the mauve top, denim shorts, and high-heeled sandals to agree. They order soy lattes to go, but then decide to sit down with them at the table that the woman with the guitar has left. The brunette sings along with the radio ("Build Me Up Buttercup" and "I Should Have Known Better") as she stirs sweetener into her latte. A thin young man with a goatee enters and joins them at the table, wearing baggy jeans, a trucker's cap, and a red t-shirt stating in white letters "Ithaca is GANGSTA."

They open up the local newspapers, pull out their cell phones, and start making calls about apartments. The black straps of the blonde woman's top, bra, and shoulder bag map out a crisscrossing neighborhood of skewed lines across the pale tan of her back.

Their table is closer to me than the counter. From this distance, I see that each of the women is bejeweled and heavily made up. The brunette's brown eyes, stunning at a theatrical distance, seem overly mascaraed from a few yards away. I wonder how her eyes would look without the makeup and suspect that I'd find them even more lovely. The blonde woman has blue eye shadow, pale lipstick, crystal earrings, and tiny golden rings and studs in the piercings on her eyebrow, nose, and lower lip.

A woman darts in from the street, holding hands with two blonde girls, perhaps two and three years old. She asks if the shop has a bathroom. "Customers only," the cashier sternly replies. "Mommy! Potty!" the younger girl loudly whines. The cashier smiles, looking defeated, and hands the woman the key.

The made-up women leave, abandoning their newspapers, though they have thrown out their trash. Looking back toward the counter, I see that a line has suddenly appeared, stretching out the door. The cashier comes out from behind the counter, bearing two large hot drinks. He guides two large, older blind women, one with a dog and one with a cane, to a table in the back.

Two more little girls, perhaps seven and eight years old, sit down briefly at the table that the made-up women had left. They sip at their Italian sodas (one green, one red), transfer some small objects among the plastic bags that they are carrying, then dart away.

As I head out of the French Hotel, I pass Cheeseboard Pizza, where a jazz trio (trumpet, piano, bass) are playing "Flamenco Sketches" for the people sitting inside, outdoors, and on the grassy median not far away. At a table, a man explains the music to a small black haired girl in a yellow blouse. "This is a song by Miles Davis, who was a great musician."

"Was he nice?" the girl asks.

"No, not nice. But he was a great musician."

4:13 PM, 31 Mar 2004

Seeing a group of cops heading down the street from Starbucks with what appear to be iced mochas with whipped cream is disorienting. The day of the donut is past, the voice of the latte is heard in the land.

Further down Shattuck, a white haired man with a trenchcoat and slightly battered briefcase spoke to a much younger man, pale with blond dreadlocks and a colorful knit hat, who sat on the sidewalk against a lamppost. The seated man had stopped his otherwise continual playing of a clay drum for the moment, and put it down between a handwritten sign begging for change and a McDonald's cup that held a few coins. "I tried panhandling here," the older man said, "but they looked at me like I was Joe Montana. I guess for folks to believe you need help, you gotta get filthy or smell bad."

3:48 PM, 1 Apr 2004

Near the center of the coffee shop, three or four flies darted about. Each zoomed in a straight line, then changed direction and flew straight again. The points at which they turned seemed to sketch a consistent cylinder, about two feet in diameter. Nothing that I could see (or, as I broached the edges of the cylinder with my outstretched hand, feel) indicated why they had chosen this column of air for their games and couldn't or wouldn't venture beyond it, but they stayed within its barriers, whether trapped or content there.

I spent about half an hour this afternoon helping the pastor and another parishioner arrange two giant palm fronds near the pulpit for Palm Sunday. Each was about 10 feet tall, far larger than any *lulav* that I had ever dealt with.

After several tries at placing and securing them, I got the idea of placing the ends of the fronds in the pit beyond the pulpit where the organist sits. I had thought of having them meet at the top as an arch, but the parishioner had the better idea of placing them so that they open outward, like arms raised in prayer.

We had difficulty securing them so that they wouldn't fall over. Fortunately, we found some useful buckets under a table in the sacristy. When I went outside to search for bricks, I discovered that two boxes of bricks, apparently from the garden, had mysteriously appeared just outside the vestry door overnight. This did the trick, and the palms are now in place and relatively stable. My only concern is whether they'll block the organist's view of the service in his rear-view mirror.

12:49 AM, 3 Apr 2004

As I did my rounds last night, the palm fronds that we had set up behind the pulpit looked almost comic. With the leaves fanning out from them and the goofy bend at the top of each, it looked as if some green giant from a Dr. Seuss book was waving from the basement.

The gardener had trimmed a lot of the trees around the church. Sawed off branches and other parts of trees lay on the ground like trophies that had come off a lodge's walls in an earthquake.

I had a very vivid dream a few nights ago of coming into the sacristy and discovering that it had been ransacked. The back door had been left open and most of the valuable secular objects (the tape deck, the vacuum cleaner, the mic stands) had been taken, but I found it maddeningly hard to tell if any of the sacred items were missing. The dream was clear enough that I had to remind myself several times the next day that it had not actually happened.

3:34 AM, 14 Apr 2004

As I walked past the church, I found several of the staff taking down some of the posters for the now-past Good Friday and Easter services. I joined them, pulling out and holding onto the thumbtacks. When one of the priests shook my hand, I quickly transferred the thumbtacks to the other hand. Stigmata would be, like, *so* last week.

When I got my usual double espresso at the corner, the barista making the drink asked if I'd like an extra shot, gratis. I declined, figuring the extra caffeine would get me running around the ceiling. A moment later, he asked if I'd like a lid. For an instant, I thought he was escalating the drug offers, until I realized he meant something to put on top of the cup.

Farther down the street a shaggy man with a long blonde beard and a fairly new looking backpack sat on a planter weaving branches with green leaves into his dreadlocks. Perhaps he meant them as camouflage. Or perhaps he was trying to accelerate a transformation into a laurel tree.

2:11 AM, 20 Apr 2004

When I did my rounds at the church tonight, I found the outdoor supply closet wide open, its light on and some of the contents, including open cases of toilet paper and paper towels, strewn about. It didn't appear to have been forced open, and the door locked again appropriately when I shut it. I couldn't tell if anything was missing. On the grand scheme of things, though, the world is probably better off if people who need to steal toilet paper that desperately are successful.

As I walked down a residential street on the way to the BART, I heard a child's voice singing what sounded like an odd medley of nursery rhymes. Getting closer, I saw a little boy in a yellow raincoat singing an arbitrary array of bits of songs: "London bridge E-I-E-I-O, pop go the weasel." When our eyes met, I smiled. He stopped singing, leaped up, and ran into the house.

A block further down, I heard two sets of footsteps come around the corner and approach me from behind. One pair of feet clacked loudly against the pavement; another pattered softly and more quickly, though they moved toward me at the same rate as the others. Looking back, I saw another boy, also about three years old and also in a yellow slicker, running as fast as he could. His mother, wearing a stylish coat and heavy-heeled boots and holding his hand, was striding beside him, easily keeping up.

I shifted to my left as they caught up with me, and they shifted to the right. As they passed, they found themselves on opposite sides of a street sign, still holding hands. When their hands hit the pole, the boy's momentum carried him completely around until he crashed into his mother's legs. "Boi-oi-oi-oi-oing!" he yelled, and fell, laughing, to the ground.

Last night, I saw one of the more pathetic street people in town. A heavy man with grey hair and beard and a filthy red parka, he is always pushing his shopping cart around the neighborhood, muttering. I have rarely seen him in one place for long—he is always either in motion or being told to move on.

This time, however, he wasn't in motion. He was sitting on a stool outside one of the fancier French restaurants in town, which was in the process of closing for the night. He sat quietly, a wooden tray table set up before him. There was nothing on the table, but I wondered if something had been or would be. Perhaps he was actually getting a meal from the restaurant, maybe made up from the still good food that they would otherwise have had to throw away while closing.

9:55 AM, 26 Apr 2004

By Bay Area standards, today's weather was close to unbearable. The temperature hit record highs in the low 90s, with the humidity of the rainy season hanging on. By the standards of anywhere that I had lived in Texas, however, the weather was spectacular.

As I walked down a usually quiet street on the way to work in the early morning, the silence was disrupted by the roar of a motorcycle. As its rider repeatedly revved the engine, she hollered to the woman standing next to her, "You can always get a noise injunction against that guy. Get a copy of the city noise ordinance and shove it under his door, and he may give you some peace and quiet." She then zoomed off into the distance. A flock of small birds who were about to land scattered to elsewhere as she drove past them.

A block further down, I passed a man who was walking a cat on a leash, trying to give it commands, which it ignored.

On the steps down to the BART, I stepped around a man sleeping on a grate. There was nothing noticeably colorful or exceptional about him: just a man in a drab blanket and hat sleeping on a layer of cardboard on a subway grate. But that situations downtown had gotten to the point that he was almost not worth noticing was worth noticing.

On the way home, I passed a young black woman with red dreadlocks pushing a purple shopping cart. A man sat in the cart, older, pale skinned, and hairless. As she pushed, he kept bellowing, "Faster! Faster!" Finally, with a roar of what sounded like frustration, she gave the cart a shove. It rolled down the slightly sloping sidewalk, steadily accelerating, until it slammed to a stop against a bus shelter. The man laughed with a disorientingly pure falsetto giggle, then went back to bellowing "Again! Faster! Again!"

3:02 AM, 28 Apr 2004

As I headed out of the vestry and down to the child care center, I found a person asleep on the landing. He (although I couldn't see him directly, I guessed that he was male from his height as he lay there) was completely wrapped in a clean-looking sleeping bag atop a plastic tarp, with a small backpack carefully placed in a corner near his head. I suspect that, rather than one of the usual chronic homeless, he may have been a traveler without a crashspace for the night, taking sanctuary in the shadow of the church. Such travelers rarely create any mess, move on after a single night, and are usually gone at dawn, long before the child care workers arrive, so I decided not to disturb him (though I may if I see him there again tomorrow night). I found the way that he had fit himself into the space, the organization of his belongings, and his gentle breathing as he slept oddly comforting, and I watched him for a while from within the hallway of the child care center before completing my rounds through the Parish Hall.

11:21 PM, 28 Apr 2004

As I passed Chez Panisse, a group of young men were balancing and adjusting a tripod that leaned far back, pointing a camera up the steps. A man came out of the restaurant and hesitated at the top of the staircase. "Come on down," one of the men called out. "We're just farting around with cameras."

I crossed the street at the crosswalk between the post office and the French Hotel. By law, vehicles must stop when they see a pedestrian crossing the road at a crosswalk (though common sense and an understanding of momentum usually keeps people from stepping into the road when a car is coming too quickly to stop). The first lane of cars, led by a motorcycle, stopped appropriately, letting me cross. As I crossed the second lane, though, a screech alerted me to a van that hadn't seen me at first, slamming to a stop a few inches from me, close enough that the wind from the car's approach ruffled my pants cuffs. I looked at the driver and smiled, which seemed to disorient her further. Neither of us could quite figure out why I had smiled.

Later, I saw a little girl trying to balance herself in odd positions on the small priory lawn. A woman in a parked car at the curb called out to her, "Are you doing yoga?" "Uh huh!" the girl called back and balanced briefly on her hands, her plaid dress dropping down and inverting itself over her face and arms, revealing deep blue cuffed shorts and pale green socks. The girl giggled once upside down and quickly fell again to earth, landing softly if inelegantly on the grass, looking like a pile of plaid and blue cloth and randomly

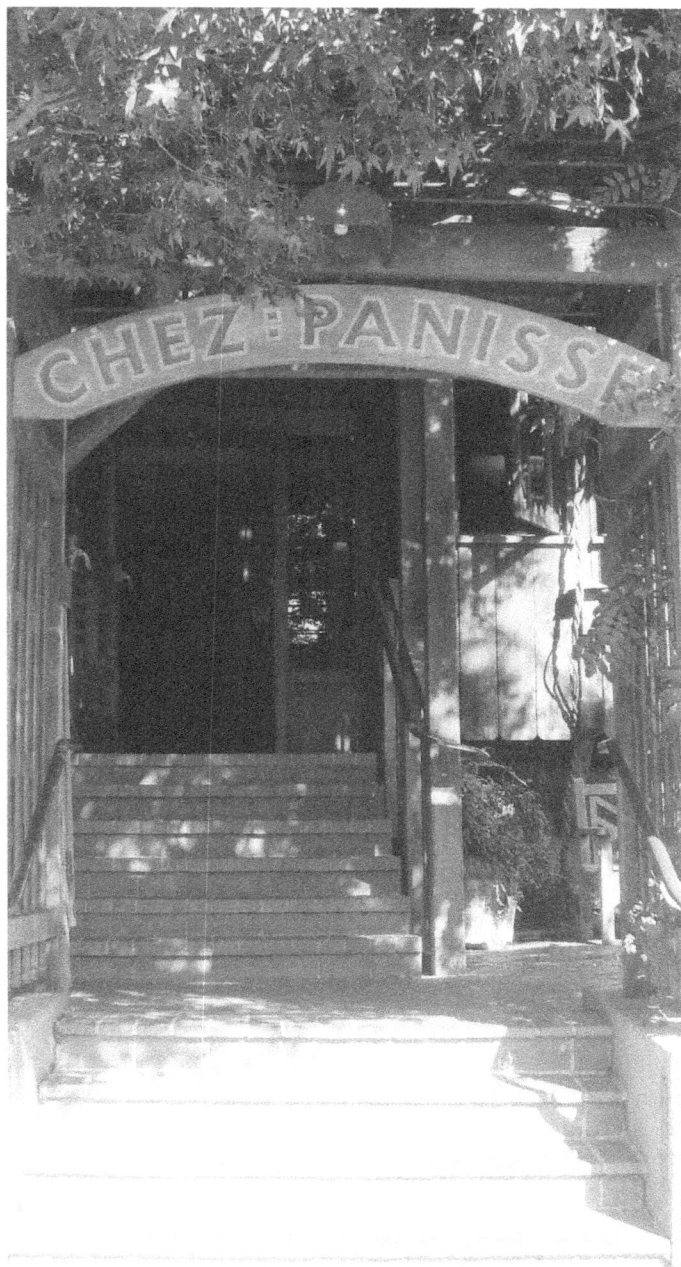

attached arms and legs until she sorted herself out and, laughing, ran back to the car.

On the way home, I was almost hit again. A bicyclist with a black pony tail, plaid skirt, and full black beard came directly at me as he escaped the path of an SUV whose driver had run the red light while talking on her cell phone. The bicyclist swerved just in time, seeming to break several laws of physics in somehow managing not to fall over or crash.

1:04 AM, 30 Apr 2004

One of the benefits of the warm weather is that people again have their windows open, which enriches the neighborhood soundscape. As on most Thursdays, the choir was rehearsing at the church across the parking lot. Odd snippets of classical music drifted out of their windows and into mine. I don't think I heard any complete pieces, but segments that they rehearsed were sung repeatedly, with unpredictable pauses between repetitions. Some of the repetitions were with the entire choir, and some were only by some of the voices. The music was further compromised and complicated by the sounds past which it came to me. The higher voices were consistently more audible than the lower, and traffic, birds, speaking voices, and other sounds masked and interwove with the choir's lines, making an odd, unpredictable tapestry of intentional and unintentional sound.

When I came down to the landing outside the church's child care center while doing my rounds, the man in the blanket was there again. He tried to wrap himself up and act as it he was asleep, but our eyes met and he knew that I knew that he was awake.

I pointed my flashlight down at him, then shifted it away so that his face was illuminated by the softer reflection of the light off the white stucco walls, rather than the painful direct glare of the light. In the vague glow I could see his white beard contrasting with his deep brown skin and, when he spoke, the very few teeth that remained in his mouth. While I could tell that he could see, his eyes seemed clouded, as if he were wearing contact lenses filled with diluted milk.

"Sir? Sir?" I called to him quietly.

He looked at me for a long moment and answered, "Yes, sir?"

"Sir, I've seen you here for two nights already, and I really can't let you stay—"

"Can I sleep one more night? I gotta be in walk-in court in the morning, and I know they're gonna take me someplace else, and I just gotta sleep one more night."

"Well, I'm the security guy for the church, and I've been told I have to tell you to leave. You know the people from the child care center saw you here this morning, and they got pretty freaked. No one is allowed down here while they're here."

"Sir, you know I got out of here the other nights I been here." Actually, I hadn't been certain of his being here more than the previous night. I knew that someone had been sleeping there the night before, but I had remembered the person differently. I started to wonder if he had indeed been here more often, arriving after I did my rounds and leaving before the people came in the morning. "Last night I don't know what happened—didn't hear my watch, and I always hear my watch, and I just slept on too late. But tomorrow I got a date in walk-in court at 9 AM, and I gotta be at the center at 7 AM so I can be clean for the court in time. So I know I'm gonna be up in time. I'm gonna hear my watch—I got it right here—" he poked a cal-loused hand out from the blanket, and moved it into the light so that I could see his cheap digital watch, rather like my own, "and I'm gonna be up in time."

I knew that I should have forced him to move on immediately, and had promised to call the police if I saw him again, but my will broke down as I looked into his pleading, milky eyes. "OK, you *have* to be out of here by dawn, and you can't leave anything behind. The child care people are quite upset that anyone was here."

"Thank you, sir," he said. "Sir, you gotta understand, I've lost everything in my life, and I was sleeping in my car, and that got towed, and there ain't no way I'm gonna get it back. And I can't go to the shelter since I'm afraid of the people there. So this is all I got. And all I need is this good dry place to sleep a night before they take me off to where they gonna take me after walk-in court tomorrow. You ever been down this far that this is all you want?"

"I...no, sir, not quite that far down. But I've been down, and I've known people where you are, and sometimes I get afraid that I might be there someday too. But—so yeah, I understand. So I'm not going to tell you to move on right away, and I'm not going to call the police. But you need to be gone at dawn, before the

child care people show up, and if you are here tomorrow night, it will be my responsibility to call the
police."

"Yes, sir, I understand. You ain't gonna see me no
more after tonight."

"OK." I swung my flashlight away so that his sleeping space was again dark, and continued on into the
child care center, carefully shielding the combination
lock from view as I typed in the numbers that unlock
it.

When I came back out of the child care center, I saw
that he was still awake and watching me, propping his
head on his hand as he rested an elbow on the ground.
"Sir?" he said when he saw that I had seen him. "Sir, I
just gotta tell you—ain't nothing in this world more
precious to me than the children, and I wouldn't do

anything to hurt none of them. The little children, I'd protect them with my life. The babies, the little three-four year olds. The five-six year olds, ain't nothing more precious. And nothing more important the Lord has given us than to make them safe, make them a good world. And I know that them women who care for them get scared, 'cause you always hear about pedophiles on the news, they always talking about them, like that fourteen year old girl in San José who got raped and escaped from the car—I know San José and I know the place they said they found her—like that fourteen year old girl they said they found in Fremont, like that girl they found but it wasn't in time and they killed her, you always hear about those pedophiles and ain't nobody sure where they hiding. Hell, you probably got some in this neighborhood but don't nobody know who they are until they grab some little girl and then only afterward the folks say, yeah, he was a creep, we knew he was. I mean, you do the security, you got your eyes open, you know about any pedophiles in this neighborhood, like you got any in a few blocks from here?"

"No, sir, not that I know of. But you can understand, with these worries, how the child care people are concerned, and get worried if anyone's here. The kids are their responsibility, and they have to be sure nothing happens to them, and that means that no one can be around who isn't absolutely supposed to be, and how they freaked when they found you here this morning."

"Yes, sir, I know, and I promise I'm gonna be long gone when they get here in the morning. What time they get here anyway?"

"I don't really know. Some days they have to do things early in the morning to get prepared for the day, so they might be here as early as six AM. I haven't figured out the schedule of what days they're here when. So you have to be out of here first thing."

"I understand. Sir, you know how it is, I care about the children, and I want to be able to be good to them as I can. But sometimes, you know, I'll be down there, sitting out by the Cheeseboard or at the glass recycling thing by the Safeway, and the little children come up to me and want to talk to me, and if they say 'Hey' to me, I'm gonna say 'Hey' to them, and their mommas run up grab them away like they afraid *I'm* one of them pedophiles, and ain't nothing farther from my mind. It just, you know, like they say, takes a village and all that."

I nodded. "I know, I have another job, and some-times kids have questions and I help them, and some-times a child needs help reaching something, and I'm always aware that a parent might get upset if someone other than them even talks to a kid. It used to be in small towns that a child was like everyone's child, and you knew that everyone was looking out to see that everyone was safe. But now everyone's scared and no one trusts anyone, so everyone always guesses the worst of everyone else. And they're right in being afraid just often enough that they keep on like that. I don't see a way out. And it's my job here doing securi-ty to keep the church and the kids safe. So even though you're a good guy and mean the best for everyone, we have to be sure you're out of here by morning."

"Yeah, I got you, and thank you."

I backed away. "OK, I have to continue checking the church. Good night, sir."

"Good night, and God bless you." He wrapped himself completely up in his blanket and rolled to face the wall, and I headed up to the Parish Hall.

1:11 AM, 1 May 2004

Rule of thumb: when you're sitting in a church, waiting for the police to force a sleeping man to move on, don't randomly pick up and start to read a sermon on the Last Supper.

The police receptionist had sounded implausibly cheerful when she answered the phone. I supposed that her job involved getting calls from an endless array of stressed and angry people all night, but she seemed to enjoy handling the phones.

I identified myself as the security guy from the church, and told her that a man was sleeping on the landing outside the child care center, even though he had been warned on previous nights not to return.

"What is the man's race?" she asked.

"What?" I replied, not expecting this to be the first question.

"What is the race of the man?" she repeated.

"Umm, he's black," I said, immediately wondering if I should have said 'African American.'

"And is he in a blanket?"

"Yes, in a yellow blanket, rolled up."

"Where is the landing? Can we see it from the street?"

"No, it's a bit hidden. If you're standing on the street,

looking at the sanctuary, it's to your right. No, your left. No, wait, right, it's on your left. To your left. And down a few steps."

"Down a few steps, to the left of the sanctuary, then."

"Right—uh, correct."

"OK, is there a number where you can be reached?"

I read them the number of the phone from which I was calling. "I'm in the Parish Office, upstairs from the landing."

"OK, Joe," she replied. "We'll send someone out, and contact you if we need to."

"Thank you." I hung up the phone and wondered how long I would have to wait.

As I sat in the office chair, I glanced around at the objects in the room. Much of it was taken up with bookcases and boxes, stashed there temporarily as one of the priests moves. On the desk, a box held a library of brightly colored flyers, each containing sermons, liturgy, and writings for the Sunday services.

By my luck, the one I picked up at random talked about the Last Supper. To an almost ludicrous level, I had sudden pangs of guilt for having called the police. Yes, I had given the man several days' grace to sleep on the landing. And yes, I had warned him that I would have to call the police if he returned, and he had promised that he wouldn't be back. But still part of me rebelled against having to disrupt this man's night, especially since there would be no one at the child care center the next morning.

I also sensed some of the ethnic humor inherent in being a Jewish guy sitting in a church and feeling guilty. But that I have this job, rewarding and appreciated as it is, is a bit nuts to start with.

I listened from within the Parish Office for the police to arrive. There were several parties happening within a couple of blocks of the church, so people were continually going back and forth to cars, arriving, departing, talking, laughing, banging doors, and playing stereos too loudly for a residential neighborhood at 1 AM.

I didn't hear the police drive up, or at least didn't recognize the sound of their car. My first sign that they were there was a brilliant glare from an industrial strength flashlight that they shone on the sleeping man.

"Yo! Yo!" one of them bellowed. "Get up and outa here! Now!"

I moved to the door, out of sight of the man and the

police, and listened. I heard the man murmur something in protest.

"Yo! What's your name?" the policeman demanded.

The man mumbled something that the policeman
echoed. Apparently the echo was wrong, since he said
it again, prompting another guess from the policeman.
This happened five or six times, until either the police
got the name right or they stopped trying.

"Yo," the policeman said, "you can sleep on the
street, or you can sleep in your car, or there's the shelter, but not the church. Nobody sleeps at the church.
You got me? You outa here?"

I didn't hear the man say anything, only the rustling
of plastic bags. The rustling went on for a long time,
while the police apparently left as silently as they
appeared.

After several minutes, the sound of the bags
stopped, and everything was quiet. I got up and continued my rounds. I didn't look down to the landing,
hoping that the police had successfully cleared the
man out, and not wanting to deal with him if they had-
n't.

As I continued through the Parish Hall, checking
doors, windows, and lights, my mind ran rapid scenar-
ios for what could have happened and what might
happen. The most dismaying prospect was also the
most probable: that I would encounter the man outside, after I left the church, dragging his bags of
belongings slowly with him. I envisioned several
responses, including ducking away entirely, pretend-
ing he wasn't there, and brushing belligerently past.

My final choice was simple. To tell him to move on

was my responsibility to the church, and I had told him that I would have to do so. If I were to meet him on the street, and he were to try to meet my eyes with his, I would look back at him and meet his gaze. I had done what I had to do, in order to keep things in order and working as well as they could in the community, and to keep my job. If he had to go elsewhere, he would have to find something, and the opportunities were known.

I didn't see him as I walked home, my worries driven away for a moment as the irresistibly cheerful voices of Beyoncé and Jay-Z blasted forth from the windows of one of the neighborhood parties. But still, as I sit here in my room, writing when I should be sleeping, I wonder about how I have disrupted the life, if just for a night, of someone whom chance and the arbitrary workings of biography happened to throw into my path.

12:19 AM, 11 May 2004

A woman pushed a man in a wheelchair down Shattuck this morning. Twice, a block apart, she stopped, threw her hands in the air, and declared triumphantly, "My name is Jambalaya!"

Outside the bakery along the way, an old man with a long white beard sat, as always, on an overturned white bucket, newspapers to his side and a plastic cup awaiting change at his feet. Today a metal chair sat across the sidewalk, facing him, bearing a cardboard sign neatly marked "SALE" and three books on investing in mutual funds.

A woman crouched over a piece of obscure machinery outside the bead shop several blocks away, brushing it carefully with a feather duster.

As I entered Starbucks, a policeman was telling the workers, "...so he just hits the guy, keeps going, then a block later pulls his truck over and calls his boss."

A barista looked up at him. "His boss? Not even an ambulance?"

"Gotta be careful about the insurance," the other worker said.

7:41 PM, 12 May 2004

John Cowan writes that he found my "mutual sir-ring" with the man in the blanket quite notable.

Thinking about this, I find that it breaks down into a weird play of power issues, in a way that Samuel R. Delany could probably go on about at incredible lengths.

I was definitely in a position of authority, there. His use of "Sir" might be read as a position of deference, using politeness as a way to seem more harmless and worthy of mercy. My use of "Sir" might be read as my using formality to hint that, while I would be merciful in not throwing him out immediately and forcibly, I still had an authority that he had to respect.

But this probably massively oversimplifies things. (And I wonder how the conversation would have been had I used the Sixties's honorific "man," rather than "Sir," in the exchange? After all, we're not far from People's Park....)

1:49 AM, 13 May 2004

Doing my rounds at the church after midnight, I sat at the piano and played a melody over and over as it grew continually simpler.

As I played, I fell asleep at the keyboard and had three dreams:

• A small brown rat looked up at me from inside the piano. I reached in, chased it down and captured it, petted it for a while as it snuggled in my hand, then opened the door to the alley and set it free.

• I was in Prague with a group of musicians. The piano was Europe. We performed by stroking, fretting, and plucking the strings near our city, running a brass slide along it for microtones.

• As I played the melody, a young girl with night-black hair and a bright blue dress sat on my knee, her head resting back against my shoulder, and sang a descant in a language that I didn't understand.

I awoke after a while, played the melody a few more times and notated it, then finished my rounds and came home, where I wrote this down so that I would remember it.

10:32 PM, 14 May 2004

I tried to do my rounds at the church early tonight, since according to the church calendar the last event was to end at 9:30, but when I finished the Sanctuary and child care center by 11 PM and went up to the Parish Hall, whatever unlisted event was going on up there was still wrapping up. So I headed home and (as I write the first draft of this paragraph) am waiting another half hour or so before I go by again. When I'm done there, my laundry should be finished in the basement here, so I'll be able to bring it up and get to sleep.

As I entered the Sanctuary, several people were unlocking their bicycles from the railing and preparing to head home. A girl with long blonde hair, which shone silver-white in the moonlight, sat on her bike waiting for her mother to unlock hers. As she waited, she sang an odd, looping melody, full of unexpected leaps and odd intervals, which repeated in ways that I could never predict. After she rode away, still singing, I went to the piano and tried to reproduce it, but couldn't get any of it down as it dissipated from memory. I wondered briefly if it was the same melody that a black-haired girl had sung in my dream in the church a few nights earlier.

In the department of Wacky Acts of God, Insurance Division: last night, the two priests from the church attended a meeting in another town. While they were indoors, a large old tree, which had never shown any signs of trouble or disease, suddenly and inexplicably came crashing down, slamming into both cars and damaging them. Anyone seriously into signs and portents might have a field day with that.

12:14 AM, 28 May 2004

We had an unusual moment here after dinner one evening last week. On the Christian calendar (at least the one that Episcopalians use; I understand that the Orthodox use one that's off by a bit), it was the Feast of the Ascension. Jane had been at a celebration of the event, and brought some of the Eucharist by for my roommates who hadn't gotten there. At our dining room table, they divided the bread (which looked more like a scone than the wafer that I had expected), and the three celebrated there. I didn't participate (being the Token Jewish Guy), though I sat at the table with them. They also poured and drank wine as part of the ceremony, and afterward (or before?) Jane and I said the Kiddush and also drank some wine.

It was quite a striking moment, particularly in how matter-of-fact it all seemed. I thought, as I experienced it, how unusual such a thing was, and how wonderful that such an event, usually imagined as happening with a lot of pomp and rigor and all the overhead that the image of The Church as a concept and institution brings to things, could happen, seemingly casually but with clear intent, at a table among friends.

11:47 PM, 29 May 2004

At the corner of University and Shattuck as I headed for the BART, a man yelled at someone we couldn't see, "I'm not going to tell you again. The ball was on the baking pan. The pipewrench is not for the ball!" The car waiting at the traffic light was blaring opera. When the man started shouting, the people in the car turned it up.

11:49 PM, 3 Jun 2004

I spent all afternoon today hanging venetian blinds in the church library. (Which is not a sentence that I ever would have envisioned myself writing.) Looking at me juggling with tools while balanced on a stepladder, the woman with whom I was working said, "You know, you're the first Jewish man I've ever met who knew how to drill a hole into a wall." She described how her late boyfriend avoided simply buying a water hose for his backyard by constructing a complex system of tubes and ditches to divert water from a stream at the far end of the property to irrigate their garden. And I thought "Yup, just the kind of thing that I would do."

Hanging the blinds was an arduous process, but with a clear learning curve: the first of the four blinds took two hours to hang, the second one hour, the third half an hour, and the fourth fifteen minutes. By which one who just looks at those numbers might guess that if we had had more to do, the sixteenth blind might have appeared in place before we even got it out of its box.

12:44 AM, 11 Jun 2004

Walking through the nave toward the narthex on my rounds Wednesday night, I heard an unfamiliar buzzing sound. When I stopped walking, the sound stopped; soon after I started walking again, the sound resumed. After several more stops and starts, I was able to zoom in on the source of the sound. Someone had placed a small table, with a glass top resting loosely within a metal frame, at the back of the church near the collection plates and flyers. The uncarpeted floor carried the vibrations of my walking up to the table, causing the stand and top to vibrate against one another.

A pack (herd? flock? family?) of raccoons crossed my path as I walked to the church from home late at night. The humans in the neighborhood had put their trash out for the night, so it was time for the raccoons to go shopping. I don't know if they noticed me. I stopped several yards away from them and let them cross, not wanting to disturb their work.

12:40 PM, 12 Jun 2004

The child care center at the church had a multi-family garage sale today. Unfortunately, I had to miss it entirely, having passed the church on my way to my other job before it had started and returned after it had ended.

When I passed the church on the way home, a series of boxes was neatly lined up on the grass in front of the child care center, containing toys, dolls, clothes and

other items. The gardener was there, cutting up some juniper bushes that other people had, with her approval, cut down a while back but had, to her dismay, never discarded. "All this stuff was in the dumpster," she said, "and I needed the space for the juniper, so I took it out and put it out for people to salvage. A woman and her daughter came by a while back and picked up some things, and the rest will probably go quickly." When I did my rounds at about 10 PM, everything but a few teacups was gone. I don't know if people had scavenged everything or if the gardener had thrown back in the dumpster whatever hadn't been taken by the time she left.

11:22 PM, 18 Jun 2004

The sonic traffic lights signal that you can cross Center Street at Shattuck by beeping a pattern, two beats out of three: high-low-silence, high-low-silence. A different pattern signals that you can cross the other way. (I can't recall what that is, though, as I write the first draft of this paragraph in my notebook while I wait for the BART. A passing harmonica player has disrupted my train of memory.)

Seated at the corner, a blond, bearded man jammed with the signals on a traverse bamboo flute. He mostly played repeating minimal figures that interlocked unexpectedly with the signal patterns. The figures occasionally launched into longer melodies that drifted above the signals before locking again into the figures or lapsing into silence.

At the post office, a small woman in a bright patchwork sweater leaned against the wall as she waited for her number to be called. "I have a Ben and Jerry's hangover," she moaned into her cell phone, "the post-chocolate slowdown, with a brain freeze that may never leave."

1:04 AM, 21 Jun 2004

There's an animal screaming somewhere in the neighborhood. At least I think it's an animal—the screeches, sliding up and down in pitch, frequently changing direction, and abruptly starting and stopping, sound like a cross between an aggrieved rabbit and a turntablist with a bad case of the shakes.

I've tried to figure out where it's coming from, but without success. The sound is so loud, and the buildings in my neighborhood are so reflective, that it bounces off of everything, seeming to switch places randomly. Come to think of it, if it's an angry mammal, it probably is in motion, and I might not want to come upon it when it's this mad. I'm a bit too tired to tramp around the neighborhood trying ad hoc echo-location.

3:05 AM, 24 Jun 2004

As I did my rounds at the church Monday night, I spotted a shopping cart full of stuff at the curb. A person wrapped in a blanket lay on the ground nearby, blocked from the strong wind by the cart and a station wagon parked on the street. Since he may not have been on church property (I don't know if the property extends past the sidewalk to the street), I let him be, after seeing some movement within the blanket that suggested that he was alive.

As of midnight on Wednesday night, the cart was still there, but the person wasn't nearby, having heaped the blanket on top of the cart and apparently headed elsewhere for a while. I'll probably call the police on Thursday and see if they or I should take some action. As usual, I'm dismayed that I may have to act to further dislodge a homeless person, but worry about the effect of his presence on the church property.

1:00 AM, 3 Jul 2004

Writing in real time: As I write this, an old man stands up from his table at the far side of the French Hotel coffee shop, jostling it off balance from its precarious position on the uneven tiles by the wall. Someone shouts, and several workers and customers surround the table, moving it and the chairs out of the way and picking up the shards of several cups and plates. Two people remain crouched where the table had been.

As the people at the table between the crash and me stand, I see that another old man, who I hadn't seen before, is seated on the floor, leaning against the wall, holding a bloody towel to the back of his head.

A fire engine and ambulance appear almost immediately. Six or seven men, in as many different uniforms, come in and surround him. I stand and look from where I had been, too far away to hear much of what is happening. What I can hear is that he has a laceration of about an inch and a half on the back of his head, and will need stitches. The firemen place a pad of gauze on the wound and wrap a turban of bandages around his head.

Asked if he wants to go to the hospital in the ambulance, he says that he wants his wife to drive him in

their car. When they help him stand, however, he wobbles and sinks back against the wall. The firemen give him a moment to regain his balance, but he stumbles immediately upon trying to take a step. Catching him, they guide him to a waiting stretcher, and roll the stretcher into the ambulance. His wife holds his hand as they roll him in. Shaking, she turns to embrace for a long moment the man who I first saw stumble, then goes to their car. The ambulance pulls away without running its siren. The man and woman, in their small sedan, follow.

On my way to work on Monday, a funeral cortege blocked traffic as it crossed Cedar Street on Shattuck. Dozens of cars, each with a black on orange FUNERAL sign on the side of the windshield closer to the sidewalk—is that the driver's side or the passenger's?

Without looking at a car in real time, I can't remember—disregarded the traffic lights, as is the custom. On either side of the stream of cars, where the two streets meet, motorcycles sat still, their riders each waving another black and orange sign at the traffic waiting for the normal flow to resume.

Getting my ritual cup of espresso at Starbucks once I'd crossed the street, I spotted a new employee. He seemed even more chipper and eager than the standard crew of somewhat hyper workers. After I got my order, I heard him exclaim to a grumpy looking customer who was eying the baked goods uncertainly: "If there's anything you want to know, just ask me!"

The customer glared up at him. "How old are you?" he grumbled.

"Thirty!" he replied cheerfully. "I was born on July 11, 1973, delivered two months early in a Caesarian. I was in an incubator for six months...."

I have no idea how long he went on after I left. I suspect that if I came back later in the day he might have been talking about what he had for lunch on his 23rd day of school in fifth grade.

Not that I have much room to complain about overly detailed verbosity :-)

A shabby man with one taped shoe was still sitting outside Berkeley Espresso, still apparently asleep, as he had been for the past several days. Looking at him, I got a sudden flash of a memory of having seen him within the sleeping bag that had been next to a shopping cart outside the church several days earlier. I had thought that I hadn't seen the sleeping man's face before. Had I forgotten that I had seen who it was, or had my unconscious retroactively assembled a spurious memory to match the face of the man asleep here?

The cart remained on the street outside the church for three days after I first saw it, the sleeping bag placed on top of it and its owner nowhere to be seen. On the third day, I finally called the police, who took my cell phone number and said they'd take a look.

After a few minutes, the phone rang. "Hey, Joe, this is the Berkeley Police. How's it going?"

"Um, OK." That was a less official greeting than I had expected.

"I'm here on the west side of the church. There's a cart full of garbage here, all right, but I've checked the grounds and I don't see anybody."

"Right. I only saw someone there a few nights ago, sleeping under it in front of the church."

"Was he on the church grounds or on the sidewalk? If he was at least partially sleeping on the sidewalk, then we can handle things."

"Yeah, I guess he was at least partially on the sidewalk. Mostly on that strip of grass between the sidewalk and the curb, but I think he was partially on the sidewalk."

"OK, then, it's in our ballpark. We can't do anything about the guy unless we actually see him, but I can send a city crew to pick up the cart."

"Um, thanks."

The police hung up. I stared at the phone for a while before I hung up too.

Was the cart full of garbage? I didn't see what was in there, within the dark plastic bags that it held, but I imagined something different, the remaining fragments of a person's life, gathered together into a few cubic feet beneath a sleeping bag that still seemed to be in quite good condition. Had they taken it to be dumped as trash, or was there any chance that they were holding it somewhere that the person could retrieve it?

The call gave me the hollow feeling that my actions might have caused a person's last scraps of material identity to be destroyed, condemning him to a final depersonalized anonymity. What might he have had in the cart: a book that he might read occasionally to sink into its better imagined world? A teddy bear saved from a distant childhood? A letter with the signature of a lost love? I tried to shake off these thoughts, telling myself that I was building a romantic fiction on top of a bleak reality.

And as I looked at the man sleeping in a chair in front of the coffee joint, where he had appeared on the evening after the cart had been removed, I wondered if it was the same person. And I wondered what he might say if he were to awaken, recognize me some-how, and know that I had had some part in destroying his last belongings.

Farther down the street, the white-bearded man was at his usual post outside the luggage shop. His cart (smaller and a lighter color than the sleeping man's) was not there. He had stood up and was rummaging through a bag. On the bucket on which he usually sat, he had been preparing a sandwich. Mayonnaise had been squeezed out in a smooth stream onto a slide of white bread. Another slice beside it held two tomato slices and some neatly trimmed lettuce. A sealed package of a pre-fab sushi platter peeked out from within the bag beside them.

I had expected the bagel shop near the BART to be mobbed. Getting there close to noon, I would usually find the place crowded with teenagers in from the high school a few blocks away. (We certainly weren't allowed to wander off-campus for lunch when I was in high school. I suspect that the administration worried that we would never return. And, come to think of it, out in the wilds of suburbia, there was nowhere near-by for us to go.)

Today, though, it was near empty. It took me a moment to realize that I had gotten out of sync with the school calendar, and everyone had fled for the summer.

A few people remained. A heavy, middle-aged man, slouching in a wooden chair, talked on a cell phone, occasionally sipping a cappuccino. A small ice cream cart sat closed next to him, its white surface covered by faded, peeling pictures of cones and popsicles and hand-written signs in English and Spanish.

At a table near the front, a couple talked eagerly, in a jargon so filled with teen buzzwords that I couldn't follow what they were talking about. (I saw today that a local bookstore is carrying a teenspeak dictionary published by the students of the local high school. I'm tempted to get one.)

The boy was neatly dressed in black. The girl wore worn army fatigues, embellished with lapel pins pro-moting anarchy and neo-punk bands. Her hair was painted orange and green, with brunette roots, and her eyes circled with so much mascara that she could have passed as an oversized raccoon. All told, she looked like a classic rebel from the 70s, straight out of *The Great Rock and Roll Swindle* or, worse, *Times Square*. I wonder if she thinks of herself as participating in a decades-long tradition, or whether her parents might have rebelled exactly as she is doing now.

Heading down Powell Street to the BART on the way home, I hear a man seated on the curb moan repeatedly "peh-hey-yi? peh-hey-yi?"—the last syllable a minor third above the first two. It takes me a moment before I can fill in the phonemes that have worn off through repetition and realize that he has been asking "Spare change, sir?"

I find myself wondering if the interval that he is singing is indeed identical to the one that figured prominently in the REO Speedwagon song that was playing in the Walgreens that I'd wandered into to get some laundry soap and a snack. And I wonder if it is because my compassion has been worn down, like his words, by the endless pleas for change, that I find myself focusing on the tonality of his cry rather than its meaning.

10:29 AM, 5 Jul 2004

On Shattuck Street, an old woman in a heavy coat stood on her toes and pulled discarded flowers from a trash barrel that was taller than she was. Stepping over to her rolling cart, she carefully arranged the flowers as a halo around the top, stuffed under the bungee cord that pressed a worn backpack down onto the pale plastic bags that filled the cart.

A grey-haired man in a plain white t-shirt and flowered shorts jogged past her, sniffling and repeatedly wiping his nose with a white handkerchief. A block ahead and across the street, six other joggers turned the corner and continued south on Shattuck, single file.

On the way home, something seemed a bit off about the color of the sky, but I couldn't pin down what. It may have been from the residue of the fireworks. It was close to midnight, and almost everything was closed. From a distance, I could hear the whistles and thuds of home fireworks and the blurred music of remote parties. Several people in capoeira gear passed me on Shattuck, turning cartwheels down the street. I headed homeward, to do my rounds, to write, and, eventually, to sleep.

1:54 AM, 6 Jul 2004

As I approach the corner of Virginia and Shattuck, I see two men staring down into the gutter. A sputtering grinding sound that I can't identify comes from the space between them. Reaching them, I see a third man crouching on the sidewalk, sawing a large board with a small electric saw. His knee holds one end of the board down onto the sidewalk near the curb. The saw is over the gutter, beyond the curb, cutting about an inch off the end of the board just past the edge of the sidewalk.

Once I pass University Avenue, I hear what sounds at first like a saxophone, then a guitar, then a full band playing loudly. The sound becomes clearer as I walk the several blocks to its source. A man in the doorway of the Kress building is playing a single harmonica, heavily amplified, his lines so complex that they form the illusion of more players.

In the gaps between his phrases, I hear what sounds like appreciative whooping from farther down the street. As I move toward it, I see that it is not related to the music. Two young men are holding a sign that, as I sit here writing a block away from the main Berkeley BART entrance, I can tell says in large letters, "Honk for," followed by whatever the cause is, written in letters too small to read from here.

Writing this, I hear the grinding of a motor approach. An electric scooter rolls toward me, and I associate the sound with that, but see that, as the scooter rides past and away, the sound continues to get louder rather than fade off. A woman follows, about a minute behind, in an electric wheelchair,

which I figure must be giving off the sound, but the grinding noise continues to get louder as she, too, passes. After a while, the noise gets almost painfully loud, then abruptly cuts off without my discovering the source. The sound of the harmonica and the whooping of the men with the sign continues in the relative downtown silence.

On my way into the BART station, I see that the sign that the men are holding says "Honk for Solar." A crew of young people are trying to get passersby to sign petitions about something having to do with solar energy, though casual eavesdropping on their fervent requests doesn't reveal more detailed information. I am amused that the people with the sign are trying to get audible endorsements of solar power from people operating gasoline engines.

1:16 AM, 9 Jul 2004

At the French Hotel, where I'm writing the first draft of this paragraph on Thursday afternoon, a tableful of boys has just left after a group tantrum. While the woman with them tried to get them to behave, the boy facing me was smashing crayons into tiny bits, the one facing away from me was waving his arms and crying, and the one in the baby carriage (wearing eyeglasses with bright blue frames) was throwing everything within reach into the air.

I didn't see what they had ordered. The French Hotel makes charming mochas and, more likely for the pre-caffeine set, hot chocolate. The barista somehow makes surprisingly detailed faces and drawings on top of the foam.

People were darting in and out as usual. One of the monks from downstairs (a near-exact clone of Charles Laughton with a deep Southern accent) wandered past toward a table in the back with a friend. Several cell phone conversations were going on at any time, mostly quite quiet.

A little girl ("I'm not five!" she told someone. "I'm five and a half!") came up from behind me and, twisting to get a good look at the Palm V and its keyboard on which I am writing this, eventually leaned against my arm and stared closely to the screen. "It's a computer," I said. "I'm writing a letter to my friends."

"Deanna!" a woman's voice said sharply before me. "Stop bothering people."

"It's OK," I said, and smiled down at the girl. She smiled back, then, spinning around on one foot, stepped back to her family's table.

Later, I heard her explain to her grandmother the aesthetics of macaroni and cheese. "You can't use Parmesan cheese! You have to use powdery cheese— little tiny pieces, tiny-winey-winey pieces, so little you can't see them. That other cheese is too big!"

12:45 AM, 11 Jul 2004

I awaken from a vivid dream: I am at the piano trying to notate a melody, but no key on the piano will
produce the same pitch twice in a row. I worry that my
melody might duplicate the music of a popular family
film. I discover that the movie composer did not write
his theme himself, but heard his six-year-old daughter
singing it. She says that she heard it from a fairy. This
I learn as a half-inch tall blue plastic bear drags a coffee cup across a shelf.

1:25 AM, 15 Jul 2004

Two people passed me, dressed in random colors,
tall cloth top hats above leather vests and contrasting
long sleeved shirts. The one nearer me played a metal
hand drum. The other, whose hands I couldn't see, was
making sounds with some sort of beads. Neither
seemed to fit any regular rhythm.

The street smelled strongly of smoke, though by the
time that I had gone another block, the smell was gone.
From somewhere nearby, a high male voice, with the
exaggerated accent of a Southerner doing a parody of
a nerdy Northerner, whined something like, "Mr Hyde!
The mice are ready for you!" From within a bus stop
enclosure across the street, a woman yelled, "You! In
the green cab! Pull over for us! Yeah, you. What, don't
stop for people like us, huh?" From her voice, I could-
n't tell what category "people like us" might be.

1:00 PM, 16 Jul 2004

I dream that one of my roommates, with whom I share a refrigerator, has asked me to store an overflow of produce in the church. Realizing that there isn't enough room in their refrigerator either, I decide that I have to eat as much of it as I can. I sit in the vestry munching on iceberg lettuce and asparagus as a group of supermodels talk shop and pass around magazines, some with fashion tips and some pornographic. I find neither interesting as they are handed to me. A radio playing in the next room plays a medley of Hootie and the Blowfish's cover of "The Goodbye Girl" and a southern rock song that I can't identify but that has the same chord changes as Dylan's "Knockin' on Heaven's Door." Radio announcers, seen in the studio in which I am then standing, discuss the medley's position on the charts, flipping through Billboard and using acronyms that I don't understand.

2:24 AM, 30 Jul 2004

I had been planning to procrastinate in doing my rounds at the church this evening, but dashed outside with my flashlight when I heard, in quick succession, a metallic crunch, a child's scream, and a grownup crying. In this neighborhood full of echoing surfaces, I wasn't able to find the source of the sounds. But once I was out, I decided to go down to the church.

It was quite warm outside, so I headed past the church to the Elephant Pharmacy to grab a soda. Standing in line, I heard a stream of giggles from behind me.

I looked down and saw a small boy grinning, giggling, and pointing at me. I tried to figure out what might be so funny, but turning in circles, I didn't see anything. I stopped, looked down at the boy, and raised an eyebrow, Spock-style.

Managing to squeeze out the words in short bursts between giggles, he exclaimed, "Mister, your...butt...is shining!"

I was baffled again, and tried to peer down to see what that could mean. Feeling behind me, though, the answer became clear. I reached into my back pocket, pulled out the flashlight, and switched it off.

The boy looked a bit disappointed that my butt stopped shining. I wondered if he had been thinking, "If ET's heart glowing means love, this guy's butt glowing means...what?"

4:16 AM, 11 Dec 2006

It's been a long time since I've encountered anyone sleeping on the grounds of the church. But now the winter is approaching with its cold winds and rain, and the homeless have begun to take refuge in its dry and sheltered nooks.

Late one night last weekend, I found someone sleeping in the east stairwell, outside the chained and padlocked door to the Child Care center. As usual, I didn't disturb him, since it was raining hard, and he wasn't blocking my path. And, as usual, he didn't return.

Two nights ago, as I passed the church at about 2 AM, in the rain again, I saw someone sleeping under the eave at the top of the western stairs to the sanctuary. The person was wrapped in a shabby yellow blanket, with a rolling suitcase standing nearby. (I've been seeing a lot of rolling suitcases over the past year. One wouldn't imagine that the people dragging them around would have a need for carry-on luggage. But the cases are getting quite inexpensive, and, I suspect, easily stolen.) Again, I didn't disturb the sleeper, sweeping the rays of my flashlight around that spot rather than over it.

Last night, passing once more at about 2 AM, I again saw the sleeper. I was tempted to take some action, since it was the second night in a row that the person was in the same spot. But it was cold and raining again, and I was too exhausted to want to deal with much of a fight, so I did my rounds as usual without doing anything about it.

I went past the church much earlier than usual tonight, at about a quarter to seven. I had been out to

dinner with my housemates, then had dropped by a nearby coffee joint for an espresso before stopping through home on the way to a performance.

Pausing for the espresso took a little longer than I expected. My predecessor, from whom I had taken over the church job almost four years ago, was sitting in the coffee shop. We almost didn't see each other, since he had his head down as he worked at a chord pattern on the electric guitar that he had running through a tiny amp to his headphones.

When he raised his head and spotted me, we got to talking briefly, with him going into one of his standard intricate trivial monologues, describing in detail why he considered the Elton John album that contained the song that he was learning to be the apex of the singer's career, and how to recognize the best of the several CD reissues of the album. Out of courtesy, I invited him to our performance that evening, but hoped that he wouldn't actually get there, since he was dressed even more poorly than usual, with holes in his flannel shirt and sweatpants.

When I got to the church, I saw that the sleeper was once again there. Since I was already running a bit late, I considered waiting until later to deal with the situation. But it was early, and the weather was relatively good, so I decided that it would be best to get the person to move on while there might have a better chance of finding a different place to crash for the night.

I climbed the stairs toward the blanket. As I got near, the sleeper rolled over suddenly and glared at me, wide eyes staring out from a pale, grimy, clean-shaven face framed and partially covered by long, stringy hair. "What?" he growled.

"Hi," I said. "I'm Joe. I do security for the church. I've seen you sleeping here for the past two nights, and we just can't let anybody get into a pattern of sleeping here. So I'm sorry, but I have to ask you to move on."

He sprang suddenly into a seated position, fully clothed except for the shoes that lay near where his head had been. "I know who you are," he muttered. "You're one of those false Christians who go killing the real people."

"Actually, no," I said. "I'm not Christian. I just work here."

That seemed to confuse him for a moment, but then his glare returned. "I know you! You're one of the satanic millennium who hang out down at the supermarket and murder priests. You're with Lady Etheridge. You're Thomas Randall, the false king of England!"

By this point, his bellow had raised to a shriek that I was certain could be heard a block away.

"No, sir. But you do have to move on."

He continued to shriek, howling insults and obscenities at me. I considered standing my ground, but realized that from where he was, he could easily shove me down the cement steps.

I stepped backward when he paused to cough. "I'm walking away now. But I will need you to be gone by the time I return. Good night, sir."

The man continued shrieking, coming up with strikingly colorful combinations of threats and obscenities.

I don't think I could repeat what he threatened to do with the bodily organs of anyone who looked like me on Christmas Day, but visualizing the image would have required a collaboration between Hannibal Lecter and Hieronymus Bosch. I ducked around the corner to the north side of the church, out of view.

Several minutes later, he was still shrieking and had not moved. I contemplated trotting back down to the coffee shop to get my predecessor for backup, but then decided that that would probably make things worse. A few pedestrians had come past and looked frightened, most crossing the street to distance themselves from the screaming.

Digging out my cell phone from my pocket, I switched it on and looked through the address book for the number of the Berkeley Police Department, which I could have sworn that I had. It wasn't there—the last time that I had had to call the police was long enough ago that I had used my previous phone. Dialing information, however, connected me to them for free.

It took a while for the police dispatcher to understand what I was calling about. I told her my location, and that an apparent vagrant who had been asked to move on was shrieking threats on the church steps. She said that she'd send someone to look into it.

As I hung up the phone, however, I heard him come down the stairs, his suitcase clanking as he dragged it down the steps behind him. The screaming didn't stop as he headed down the hill away from me.

I called the police again to tell them that he had moved, but might still be a problem. I confused the dispatcher by telling her that he was moving south on what turned out to be an east-west street (for some reason, my mind tends to map 'downhill' to 'south'), but when I told her that he was moving away from a particular street and toward another, she figured out what I meant. But by the time that I got off the phone, I couldn't hear him anymore. I didn't know whether he had finally stopped screaming or just moved out of earshot, but I wasn't going to follow him and find out.

I walked on, disturbed, but less shaken than I would have expected. This was the first time that someone that I had encountered in this situation had turned out to be this aggressive and deeply disturbed, and the first time that I had been threatened.

When I returned to do my rounds at about midnight, all was clear. He hadn't returned, and no one else had taken up any of the shielded dry places along the perimeter of the church.

I'll keep an eye out for him. But my hunch is that he may quickly forget me and that this ever happened, and will keep moving on, slogging across the intersections between our mundane (if soggy) streets and the horrific world that he seems to perceive.

7:20 AM, 7 May 2007

A vagrant who spent a luxurious night in our posh Library Suite is now under arrest and headed for less comfy accommodations in jail. Nothing appears to have been damaged and nothing was taken.

I came through the Parish Hall in the course of my rounds at about 1:50 this morning. When I entered the library, I spotted someone (black, male, in his twenties or so, wearing a t-shirt and boxer shorts, with other clothes folded neatly on the floor) on the couch, as if asleep but with eyes wide open. I identified myself and asked who he was. He said nothing, but continued to stare at me. I told him that he had to leave, and asked if anyone had said that he could stay there. He did not respond.

I told him that I would be right back, and headed quickly home to see if there was an email given a reason why he might be there. I also checked my phone messages, realizing that I hadn't turned my cell phone on after leaving my other job (at which we have to leave all cell phones turned off).

There was a message from one of the people who rents an office, saying that she had found someone riffling through papers in the building when she came in. The person did not respond to questions. The renter called the Rentals Coordinator, who directed her to me.

I returned to the church and told the man in the library that he had to leave. He slowly got up, went into the bathroom and used it, came back into the library, and lay down again on the couch. When I continued to question him, he only muttered one line. I couldn't tell if it was in English. I told him that I was calling the police, and headed outside to avoid a personal confrontation.

I called the police at 2:02 AM, and gave the information to the dispatcher. She said that it would take a while for the police to get there, since there had just been a major incident in which two firefighters had been stabbed.

I ended up waiting outside for almost five hours (checking again with the police after two hours, at which point the same dispatcher said that everything was very backed up). I listened continually for indications that he had left by either the main, kitchen, or meeting room doors. I ducked into the building once—realizing, at about 5 AM, that I was starting to fall asleep, I nabbed a copy of John Mabry's *God has One Eye* from the Sacristy to read to keep me awake. (Imagine: sermons that actually keep people awake!)

A policeman finally drove up at about 6:45. It took a few tries at explaining to get through to him that the guy was actually *inside* the building—but once he realized that, it made his plan of action a lot easier. I opened the main Parish Hall doors for him, and showed him (from outside) that the Library was at the end of the hall.

He went in and, a while later, emerged with the sleeper, who was now dressed, handcuffed and carrying a bag. The policeman frisked him and guided him into the car, then brought the bag back to me to check if anything within it had been taken from the church. It appeared that nothing was (assuming that we're not using beat-up looking gangsta rap CDs in any of our work). He told me the guy's name, and he had an outstanding ten thousand dollar warrant. They drove off into the sunrise. (The first sunrise that I've experienced, by the way, in a very long time—the soundscape is amazing when sitting quietly outdoors!)

I double-checked the Parish Hall to make sure that everything was secure. (Fortunately, no one from Child Care had arrived yet, so they didn't have to be factored into the situation.) After indulging in some goodies that one can only get from the Cheeseboard bakery very early in the morning, including their very good espresso (necessary fuel for writing this up), I came home.

And now for three or four hours of sleep, then off to the other job.

6:13 AM, 18 May 2007

Most of the time, my stuffed Linux penguin, Tux, gazes benevolently from my window onto the busy intersection below. He's usually happy to stay there, but apparently wanderlust got the better of him this evening.

I did my rounds as usual tonight, getting to the church at about 1:45 after having gotten off my other job at half past midnight and caught the first All-Nighter bus home.

The rounds were mundane. Nothing seemed out of the ordinary for much of it. No doors or windows had been left open, and no one was asleep on the grounds. (On the previous night, a young, polite man was lying on the church steps when I arrived, gazing at the sky, his head resting on his backpack. I introduced myself as the security guy and said that, while he could continue to enjoy the night sky, he couldn't fall asleep there. By the time I looked out of the narthex onto the steps a few minutes later, he was gone.) Someone had tucked what looked like an infant's cap into the handle of the door of the child care center, but everything else there seemed OK.

When I came up out of the child care center, however, a spot of bright yellow caught my eye. Looking more closely, I saw Tux, nestled comfortably at the

corner of a flower bed where I'd be sure to see him, secure by a sturdy drainpipe. I was, of course, surprised.

Assuming that my Tux was still at his post in my window, I realized that this might not be my penguin. Here in Berkeley, there are lots of Linux enthusiasts (though major figures in one of Linux's friendly rivals in the field of UNIX-like systems, BSD, live across the street). He was the right size, but I couldn't recall whether my Tux wore the lapel button that this one had. I decided to pick him up and take him with me. If, when I looked up at my window, my Tux was still there, I would put him back by the drainpipe.

I completed my rounds through the parish hall with this Tux nestled in the crook of my arm. He accompanied me through the halls as I turned the appropriate lights on and off, shut blinds that had been left open, stepped onto the back balcony and scanned the playground with my flashlight, walked the perimeter of the labyrinth checking that the windows were shut, and checked the doors and windows of the kitchen.

Coming around from the church driveway and back onto the street, I looked up at my window and saw that Tux indeed was not there. I had apparently left the window open, and he must have plummeted out. Fortunately, a two-story fall isn't too hazardous for a well-stuffed plush bird, and neither dogs nor rain nor gloom of night seemed to have bothered him at all.

How he got to the church, however, was a mystery. The street between my home and the church is hazardous, and, even if a six-inch penguin were to take it upon himself to waddle across, he might not understand traffic lights, and would probably not be seen by the cars. Even then, he would have had to have known to go the church, hopped up a couple of feet onto the flowerbed, and positioned himself where I would see him.

More likely, of course, is that a human helped him. Whoever it was would have to have spotted him on the ground, recognized where he came from, known that the window was mine, known that I worked at the church, and placed him where I was likely to find him.

Tux is home now, sitting on my lap as I write this. He will resume his post at the window soon, but I will be more conscientious about keeping him from falling out the window.

The senior pastor at the church speaks frequently of "miracles of grace" that keep happening there. This is another, even if it is only (only?!) grace, however you define it, moving a kindly person to help a prodigal stuffed bird to return home. For this, much thanks.

1:41 AM, 27 Feb 2007

Word is apparently spreading of the congregation's friendliness to animals, even of the stuffed variety. (I wonder if Tux has WiFi enabled.) A pair of teddy bears have appeared, nestled against the main doors to the Parish Hall. From their garb, they are apparently waiting to be married. I'm not sure, however, if California allows a human pastor to perform the ceremony, so we may have to consult our legal eagles (assuming that the birds do not turn out to be stuffed turkeys).

The bears appear to be safe from the rain, so I left them there to be greeted by someone who might know where they might actually belong.

2:11 AM, 28 Feb 2007

When I did my rounds tonight, I found the bears still outdoors. They looked like they'd been knocked around a bit, and the one in the tuxedo had lost a shoe.

I've granted their pleas for sanctuary, and have placed them on the great table in the nave, where they are gazing upon the tall cross and multicultural flags and, I hope, feeling warm and safe. Perhaps someone who comes to the Wednesday event tonight will be able to discern what further to do with them.

(Addendum: On May 7th, the church treasurer wrote: "The bears are still coming to Sunday morning services. We'll let you know when they finally get around to asking for a wedding ceremony. Undoubtedly they'll want you to be their Best Man!")

Epilogue
10:06 PM, 27 Sep 2008

At the end of August 2008, I left Berkeley. The Priory where I lived had passed on to another order of monks, and the guest housing had closed down. After a bit of looking, I moved to Cleveland, Ohio, to start a communal Jewish arts collective.

Over the years, the rounds settled into a set routine. In fact, I had to do little tricks every so often to reawaken myself to the task, such as doing the rounds backwards, or counting instances of a particular detail.

I only unexpectedly missed doing the rounds twice in those years (once when ill, and once when I had stayed too long at a gathering in San Francisco, missed the last BART train, and couldn't quite figure out the obscure connections needed to get back to Berkeley by bus). When I've taken my rare vacations, and when I went back to New Jersey when my father passed away, my roommates and the church's parishioners covered for me. Fortunately, still being a technical writer at heart, I had documented the rounds in extreme detail as soon as I was comfortable in doing them.

Much of the interior of the church has been redesigned. What had been called the gym is now the Labyrinth Space, with a Chartres-style labyrinth painted on the floor (which I occasionally would walk, late at night, when in need of contemplation). The sanctuary has new paint and carpeting, and the pews and other furniture have been shifted so that the service is led from a table at the center of the space (which I had suggested, reminded of the organization of many

Orthodox synagogues). Renters of the various spaces have come and gone, and the calendar of events is always changing, so I ended up spotting unlocked doors or similar issues a few times a month.

While my predecessor had warned me of a long list of dangerous people who would break into and attack the church, I never had trouble with any of his nemeses. I tried to deal gently with the people that I encountered, and they seemed to return that respect.

It took a while for the congregation to find another person to do the rounds. Worried that one might not be found, I got ahold of a small video camera and created an impromptu training video. Fortunately, a good person was found just in time, and I was able to train him briefly. I trust that he'll do well.

I'm sitting now in a coffee shop outside Cleveland, seeing a few people wander down a city street, busier than Cedar, quieter than Shattuck. As midnight approaches, I still find a bit of me watching the clock, instinctively ready to get up, pull out my flashlight and keys, and wander about the silent church.

That part of my life has passed now, and I've moved on to new excitements and new challenges. But surprisingly often, when I close my eyes at night, I feel myself moving through a memory of the church, checking for people, listening for other creatures within the walls.

So if there is a place where memory, dreams, day and night, the present, past, and future, the sacred and the mundane all meet, our spirits may sense each other over the thousands of hours and of miles. And we'll all see each other on the rounds.

About the Author (right)

JOSEPH ZITT's writings and recordings emerge from decades of experience with computer systems, religious studies, and vocal improvisation. His other books include *Surprise Me With Beauty: The Music of Human Systems* and *Shekhinah: The Presence*. After a career as a technical writer and programmer, he now works as a bookseller and lives in a communal Jewish arts collective outside of Cleveland, Ohio.

About the Photographer (left)

CHELSEY. E. STEWART's heart belongs to the photographic image from concept to execution. A graduate from the Academy of Art University in San Francisco, she embodies the desire to capture the creative essence of the moment as well as the personal connection and vision of those who inspire her.